Introduction

You know . . .

Rim job.

Eating ass.

Tossing the salad.

Anilingus (we are going to use the fancy, official word here since we are very fancy and official) is clearly nothing new. Even the formal term has been around since 1899, with the English translation of sexologist Richard von Krafft-Ebing's 1886 book *Psychopathia*

The food pyramid according to Gen Z

sexualis (great book for your collection if you are a sexology nerd, btw).

Ok, physiology 101. The anus is the opening where stool (poopie) leaves the body. The rectum just above it is what connects the anus to the colon. While the default mode of most muscles in the human body is relaxed, the default mode of anal muscles is tense.

The anus is comprised of both internal and external anal sphincters, which are strong rings of muscle that are designed to protect one from shitting one's pants on the regular. Which is a system that works pretty well most of the time. And this all relates to anilingus more than you might first expect.

The anus has a bunch of nerve endings, enough to make it a legit erogenous zone. The different types of nerve endings in the bootie-butt have actually been studied. Meissner's corpuscles recognize touch sensations in general, Krause end-bulbs notice temperature changes, and both the Golgi-Mazzoni bodies and pacinian corpuscles respond to friction (tension and pressure changes). Then the epithelium itself (the cell layer that lines the colon) has a good number of thick (large diameter . . . that's what *she* said) free nerve endings throughout. All of these nerve pathways are branches of the sacral roots of our spinal column (S2 through S4).

So butt stuff? Really does feel good for a lot of people. A study published in *The Journal of Sex Research* in 2016, looked at the sexitimes of 40,000 married and cohabitating couples and found that 30% of them had engaged in anal stimulation, which encompasses all forms of anal sex, including anilingus . . . so you aren't alone if this is what you are either into or curious about.

How Does All This Work Then?

For the most part, anilingus is similar regardless of genitals. One major difference is that if you were born with a penis you were likely also born with a prostate. Prostate stimulation can be super pleasurable (as discussed in my book *Unfuck Your Blow Jobs*) in-and-of-itself and anilingus lends to that.

Additionally, if you were born with a penis, you likely have more inside area to play with, because you don't have as many organs in that area as someone who was born with a vulva.

Everyone has varying degrees of hair and odor (polite things to keep under control if you are a receiver) and everyone has varying levels of muscle strength (meaning tightness of the sphincter muscles).

Technique

Anilingus involves any use of the mouth or tongue to stimulate all of those nerves in the anus. Kissing, licking, or wiggling the tongue around the edge of the anus as well as further inside of it. Everyone is different in terms of the sensory stimulation they enjoy, so have conversations, give feedback, and if you are the giver pay attention to how your partner responds.

Anilingus can involve a variety of techniques to stimulate the anus, including kissing or licking; it may also involve the tongue moving around the edge of the anus or up and down the insides of the cheeks of the buttocks, and in and out of the anus.

If this is new for the receiver, start with lots of teasing. Massage your partner's inner thighs, their lower back, their glutes. Start with short, light tongue strokes. You can use a (lubricated!) finger or toy to help them relax by running it lightly over their anus and then in light circles just inside their anus, before moving into stronger pressure and deeper penetration.

Like everything else, pay attention to how your partner responds and also ask them what they are enjoying/ want more of and are less into / want less of.

If your partner has a prostate, they may really enjoy some prostate stimulation, with a toy or your finger. While having an orgasm from anilingus alone isn't super frequent (but does happen, which is awesome if that's you), adding prostate stimulation can help push your partner over the edge.

The prostate is a gland the size of a walnut that lies underneath the bladder. It helps the body make seminal fluid and helps keep sperm alive for baby making and it can definitely aid in having quicker and stronger orgasms.

You can stimulate the P spot either externally or internally. Externally involves pressing/tapping/ massaging the perineum. The perineum is more often referred to as the gooch, grundel, or the taint. The taint being my personal southern favorite...it taint the penis and it taint the ass.

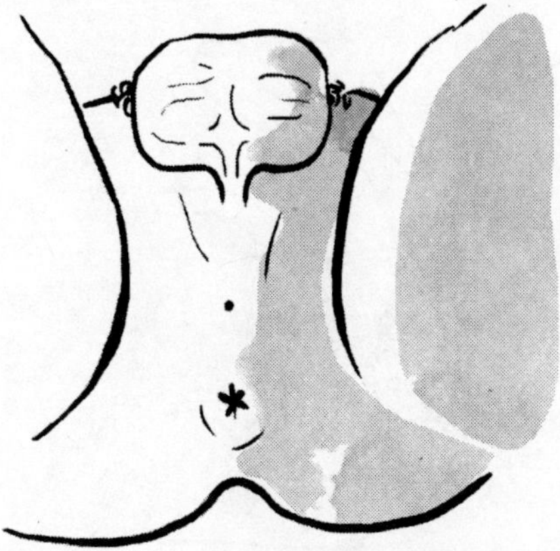

If you want to stimulate it more directly, that requires penetration either with a finger or a prostate massaging sex tool. The P spot is about two inches up inside the anal canal portion of the rectum. If you have generally average length fingers, that's about as deep as inserting to your first knuckle.

When talking specifically about anilingus, the position you choose should also be as much about comfort as access. Doggy style, with the giving partner on the outside of the doggy-pile gives the easiest access, but may be tough on the receiving partner's knees.

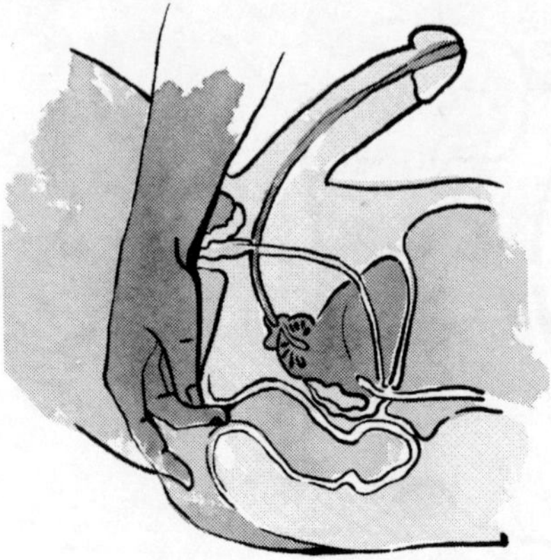

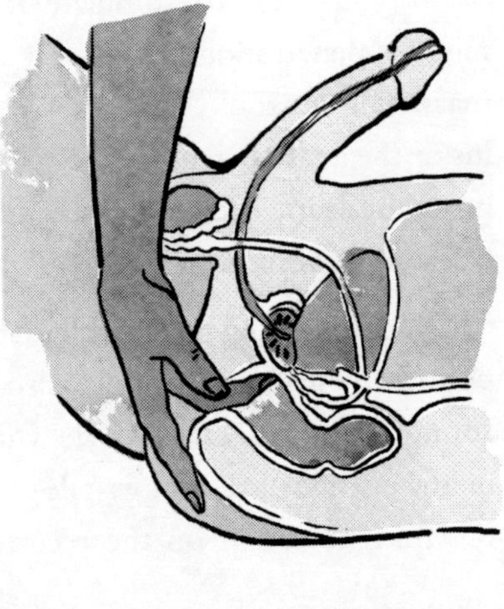

Missionary style with hip support (wedge pillows, etc) can allow the receiving partner to lift the buttocks up enough that neither partner has to take on a lot of pressure on their joints.

The 69 position, or just sitting on the receiving partner's face, works as well for anilingus as it does for fellatio and cunnilingus. If it's comfortable for the giving partner, it gives more experiential control to the receiving partner, since they can move up and down, gyrate, etc.

If you want to go super fancy? There is a position called *the rusty trombone.* The receiving partner needs to have a penis for this (equipment issued at birth, biocontructed, or store bought all work equally well). They stand in front of the giving partner, who from a kneeling position performs anilingus while stimulating the receiver's penis with their hand or hands from behind. This (very loosely) resembles someone playing the trombone.

Help, I Can't Relax My Butt!

If you struggle with relaxing the sphincter muscles enough to enjoy the sensation, you may need a little more time and a little more teasing/foreplay to relax. A couple other things that can help?

1) This was mentioned earlier as part of anilingus foreplay, but this is also something you can do for yourself (if you have the mobility to do so). Using a finger or a smaller dilater with some lubricant. Insert gently and move it gently in circles until your nervous system recognizes this as an enjoyable sensation and ceases clenching. Because the anus doesn't have natural lubrication, using a lube specific for anal play can also be very helpful.

2) Practicing kegels will help your level of control with the whole downstairs system in general, including sphincter muscles.

3) A breathing technique that is relaxation focused will also help. The default mode of these muscles is

tenseness, right? So relaxing them is an active process. Breathwork that helps relaxation is any breathwork where your outbreath (parasympathetic) is longer than your inbreath (sympathetic). Try breathing in for 2 and out for 4. If you have the lung capacity, in for 4, hold for 7, and out for 8 works really well. Pretend you're breathing through a straw while you're doing this, which can help you control your breath flow more easily.

If none of the above works, it's ok. You are not a failure, this may just not be for you!

Kegels

Being healthy is far easier if we exercise, right? Sexual health has its own exercise...the Kegel. Obviously, Kegels aren't magically curative for all kinds of sexual disorders but they are one of the go-to exercises that really help a lot of people! Kegel exercises are designed to strengthen the pelvic floor muscles, focusing specifically on the "PC" (pubococcygeus) muscles. Kegels have tons of practical use for all kinds of issues, whether you have a vagina or penis.

Dr. Arnold Kegel was a gynecologist who developed these exercises for people who had pelvic floor weakening post-childbirth. He found another interesting side benefit: His patients who were doing kegels regularly were achieving orgasm with greater ease and frequency, and had a more intense experience, showing that kegels have an additional benefit to sexual intimacy. They have been found to help both women and men better achieve orgasm, and can help both sexes feel more in control of their sexual experience for a few reasons:

- Kegels help control urinary incontinence, so many individuals feel more secure during sexual activity and less likely to leak urine.

- Kegels help give the individual on the receiving end of penetrative intercourse more control over the experience and more intense orgasms. They also create a tighter vagina or anus, therefore increasing the pleasure of the penetrating partner as well.

- Kegels help bring more blood flow to the pelvic region in women and the perineum region in men, potentially intensifying your arousal.

Kegels can be done with or without an aid (such as a dildo, vibrator, or tool designed specifically for Kegel mastery like Betty Dodson's kegelcizer). They can be done solo (which is usually a good place to start) as well as during penetrative intercourse (which can be a lot of fun for both partners).

Here's how to do them:

• Locate the muscle group in question by squeezing the muscles you use to stop your urine flow. If you are urinating and are able to halt the flow, you have the right muscle group. Your stomach and buttocks muscles should not tighten in the process. You also don't want to do your kegel exercises when emptying your bladder on a regular basis. That can lead to weakening the pelvic floor muscles which can prevent you from fully emptying your bladder (which, in turn, can lead to an increase in urinary tract infections).

• If you are using a kegel aid, lubricate the aid before insertion and practice kegels lying down. If you are not using an aid, it may be of benefit at first to practice lying down.

• Squeeze the muscle group for three seconds, then release for three seconds. Complete 10 to 15 cycles of squeeze and release.

• Try to do this at least three times a day. The more regularly you perform the exercise, the better results you will get (just like any exercise).

As you get more comfortable doing this, you will find that you don't have to set aside "kegel time" to be effective. You can do them while engaging in other activities since no one will know what you are up to—unless of course you are doing them during sex, in which case your partner will know and appreciate it!

Safety Precautions

So first off, yes. Yes, anilingus does have a higher risk of oral contact with human feces. Which means the potential for the following disease transmissions:

- Bacterial infections like shigellosis (bacillary dysentery)

- Viruses like heps A[1], B, and C, poliomyelitis, herpes, and human papillomavirus (HPV)

- Intestinal parasites

- Sexually transmitted infections like chlamydia and gonorrhea

- Gastroenteritis

- Conjunctivitis (pink eye!)

- Lymphogranuloma venereum (I had to look this one up. Y'all. This is a different form of chlamydia bacteria than the one we associate with genital chlamydia. It causes a chronic infection of the lymphatic

1 Rarer, happens only if the receiver had eaten contaminated food which is then present in their fecal matter. But still.

system and that sounds awful. I don't want any of us getting that.)

- Parasites[2]
- E-Coli (if the giver places their mouth onto the urethra of the receiver after it being on the anus) which can need to a very gnarly UTI

HIV, at least, is not believed to be easily transmitted through anilingus, though tears in the anus and tears in one's mouth could lead to transmission from giver to receiver and vice versa. So let's not test the gods on that one either, eh?

Now, if you are new to the idea of anilingus, let me add a bit more anatomy here. We aren't talking about sticking your tongue into a pile of literal shit. Feces doesn't sit in the anus, but sits in the sigmoid colon. And even if you have an impressive lizard tongue, you aren't going up that far. The sigmoid colon collects and stores all the poopie until it fills up enough that the

---

2 Also on the rarer side, but if the receiver has eaten undercooked meat, that could lead to the consumption of parasites that become present in the fecal matter

pressure tells the body to express it out (take a shit). So we are talking about small amounts of fecal debris still sticking around (pun absolutely intended). And cleaning yourself will help a lot of that.

So clean your bootie-butt. Not just wipe clean. Soap-and-water clean. At least a baby wipe clean if you don't have access to a shower. Some people will give themselves an enema to feel super clean and so they don't have to worry about feeling any pressure to go use the bathroom during.

I'm not going to tell you not to, I know it's a fairly widespread practice for people that engage in anal play more regularly. But, keep in mind that *rectal enema injuries* happen often enough that the acronym REI exists in medical literature. Both mechanical trauma and chemical irritation are both possible, causing damage or death of the tissues in the area. And in rare cases causing Fournier's Gangrene (FG), a life threatening form of gangrene that is specific to the perineum.

So Auntie Faith wants you to be extra careful, please. She would greatly prefer you to not use chemical enemas. And if you do give yourself an enema, do so several hours before sexitimes so the inflammation settles somewhat and if you accidentally hurt yourself you have time to notice. Auntie wants you to stick around for a long, long time having lots of fun, sexitime adventures, ok?

Everyone has hair down there, unless you wax on the regular, and hair provides its own protection to sensitive areas. But keeping it trimmed and clean is also important, you will be far less likely to drop dingleberries all over the place.

Don't brush your teeth for a couple of hours before or after engaging in oral activities. Those little microbleeds in our gums can lead to increased risk of disease transmission. While we are focusing mostly on giver to receiver, bleeding gums increases the chances of passing on an infection from receiver to giver, as well. You can, however, gargle with a mouthwash or even hydrogen peroxide to freshen your breath. And, especially if you have multiple partners, use barrier protections. Use a sex dam for anilingus and a different, clean, dam or condom for when you switch over to genitals so you aren't spreading potential infectors around.

While condoms cannot be DIY'd, sex dams can! Condoms can be cut open (and while you don't want to use a spermicidal condom for oral sex, you can use one for a dam conversion, so long as the spermicidal part isn't where your mouth is going).

Disposable gloves (which make manual sex safer on its own) can also be converted into a dam by cutting off the fingers and then cutting open the palm of the glove along one side and unfolding it. But even easier? Saran Wrap as a barrier dam has proven to be effective in the prevention of the spread of STIs. Super easy.

Another trick I picked up from the Scarleteen website about sex dams is to write a non-reversible letter, number, or symbol on one side of the dam so you don't accidentally reverse the dam later during play.

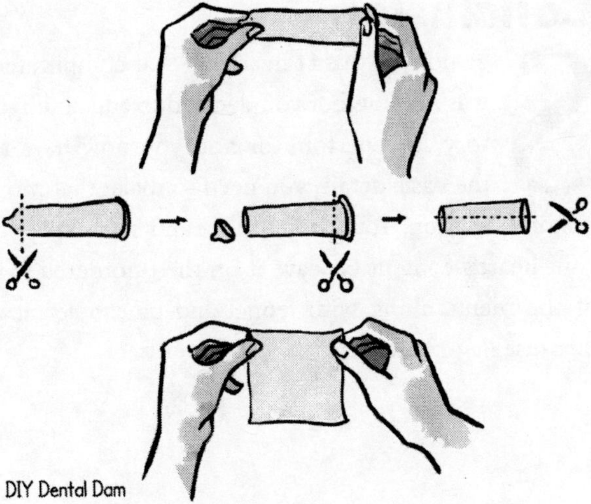

DIY Dental Dam

Dental dam
(used on vagina and anus)

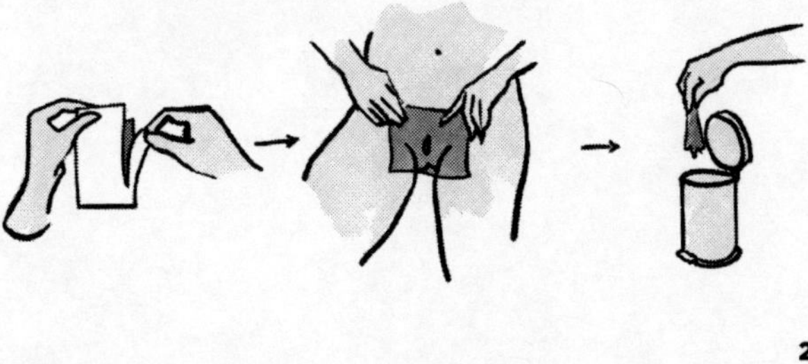

Conclusion

See now? It wasn't nearly all that complicated, was it? Whether you decided to add anilingus to your repertoire or not, you now have all the basic details you need to make that more mindful decision. You can joyfully (and safely) play to your heart's content or leave it on the unordered part of the menu, along with fennel and pineapple pizza (because *that's* nasty).

References

Anilingus. Anilingus - an overview | ScienceDirect Topics. (n.d.). Retrieved January 17, 2022, from https://www.sciencedirect.com/topics/biochemistry-genetics-and-molecular-biology/anilingus

Frederick, D. A., Lever, J., Gillespie, B. J., & Garcia, J. R. (2017) What Keeps Passion Alive? Sexual Satisfaction Is Associated With Sexual Communication, Mood Setting, Sexual Variety, Oral Sex, Orgasm, and Sex Frequency in a National U.S. Study, The Journal of Sex Research, 54:2, 186-201, DOI: 10.1080/00224499.2015.1137854

Glehn, M. P., Ferreira, L. C., Da Silva, H. D., & Machado, E. R. (2016). Prevalence of Trichomonas vaginalis and Candida albicans among Brazilian Women of Reproductive Age. Journal of clinical and diagnostic research : JCDR, 10(11), LC24–LC27. https://doi.org/10.7860/JCDR/2016/21325.8939

Kubota, T. (2017, December 4). A once-taboo sex move goes mainstream. Men's Journal. Retrieved January 17, 2022, from https://www.mensjournal.com/health-fitness/anilingus-really-w201997/

Liang, Y., Di Re, A., & Ctercteko, G. (2020). Iatrogenic rectal injury associated with fleet enema administration masquerading as Fournier's Gangrene. Journal of surgical case reports, 2020(2), rjz414. https://doi.org/10.1093/jscr/rjz414

Nichols, J. S. (2015, May 30). Do you brush your teeth before or after eating ass? - everything is sex. LTASEX. Retrieved January 19, 2022, from http://www.ltasex.com/home/do-you-brush-your-teeth-before-or-after-eating-ass/2015/5/30

Rectum, anus, and anal sphincter. MyHealth.Alberta.ca Government of Alberta Personal Health Portal. (n.d.). Retrieved January 17, 2022, from https://myhealth.alberta.ca/Health/pages/conditions.aspx?hwid=str2218&

Rogers J. (1992). Testing for and the role of anal and rectal sensation. Bailliere's clinical gastroenterology, 6(1), 179–191. https://doi.org/10.1016/0950-3528(92)90026-b

PESTS UNITE!
MICROCOSM PUBLISHING.COM